Praise for *Dancing at the Gate*

"I have had the privilege of treating Carol for years. Carol is tenacious and a seeker of truth. During our visits, she was like a detective searching for clues. Clues, in her case, to solve a chronic illness that she wasn't going to let control her life. I am honored and humbled to partake in her care and journey for relief. I think this book is a fabulous guide of willpower."

—M. Shazad Wada, MD
Anesthesiologist, Interventional Pain
Management
Pain Physicians of Atlanta

"Knowing Carol since her journey with chronic pain began, I can only marvel at how her love for the Lord and assurance in His sovereignty has grown. And now she shares wonderfully the source of her hope. As a physical therapist for over forty years, I have come to know where our true healing begins. Carol has drawn a beautiful path for us to follow."

—Jodi Rowe
Therapy Clinic Director, Motion PT
Trinity Springs, a Faith-Based Senior Care
Community

"Thank you, Carol, for opening your heart to Spirit-led praying, and now, for sharing with us what has been imparted to you. As you said about one of the Scripture passages, your book is truly a short course in how to live each day. Each day, someone who dances at the gate with you will be fed or led to the wisdom, excellent questions, and love you so beautifully gift to us."

—Phil Miglioratti
Pray.Network Curator/Coordinator

Dancing at the Gate

Dancing at the Gate

Facing Pain with Hope and Courage

Carol K. Grosz

Heavenly
Light Press

Alpharetta, GA

ISBN: 978-1-63183-529-2 - Paperback
eISBN: 978-1-63183-530-8 - ePub
eISBN: 978-1-63183-531-5 - Mobi

Printed in the United States of America   090721

♾This paper meets the requirements of ANSI/NISO Z39.48-1992 (Permanence of Paper)

*For my mother, Rose, who taught
me the song of words.*

Acknowledgments

I am grateful for all of the hands that bless me. Because of you I am no longer a cripple or a beggar but a dancer at the gate of my life. And it's beautiful. I especially want to thank my husband Sandor Grosz, my beloved sister Jeri Greene, Ann Lindgren, Dr. Shazad Wada, and Michele Chen, ANP, BC.

Introduction

Do you and I share a burden? Perhaps you or someone you love spends weary days and nights struggling with health problems. Is it fear, is it despair, is it a longing that surpasses all words? Will this cup of suffering ever pass? Where do we turn for the conviction and the strength to continue?

For over twenty-five years I have shared my life with a neurological pain disease. Like so many Chronic Pain Warriors, I fight the daily battle to hang on to my faith, my sanity, and my serenity, even my place in my family. It seems at times that the struggle to maintain some semblance of order is beyond my capabilities.

And it is.

These selections of Scripture focus on God's

promises. He promises not to forget. He promises to share His strength. These words of Scripture are reminders of how faithful He has always been. For me, these holy words represent survival.

As we remember the blessing of our daily lives, let's not forget the people who pray for us. Let us not forget to pray for our doctors, therapists, and all of the loved ones who participate in our care.

And for all of you who pray for us, for loved ones who serve us and lend your strength, it is my fervent hope that these selections will speak to your heart, too.

Dancing at the Gate Called Beautiful

"One day Peter and John were going up to the temple at the time of prayer—at three in the afternoon. Now a man crippled from birth was being carried to the temple gate called Beautiful, where he was put every day to beg from those going into the temple courts. When he saw Peter and John about to enter, he asked them for money. Peter looked straight at him, as did John. Then Peter said: 'Look at us.' So the man gave

them his attention, expecting to get something
from them.

"Then Peter said: 'Silver or gold I do not have, but
what I have I give to you. In the name of Jesus
Christ of Nazareth, walk.' Taking him by the right
hand, he helped him up, and instantly the man's
feet and ankles became strong. He jumped to his
feet and began to walk. Then he went with them
into the temple courts, walking and jumping and
praising God. When all the people saw him walking
and praising God, they recognized him as the same
man who used to sit begging at the temple gate
called Beautiful, and they were filled with wonder
and amazement at what had happened to him."

The Book of Acts 3:1–10

NIV

"Trust in the Lord with all your heart
and lean not on your own
understanding; in all your ways
acknowledge him, and he will make
your paths straight."
—Proverbs 3:5–6
NIV

Just what *is* our understanding of our circumstances? We live with serious and significant issues. Very serious. Yet no matter how much desolation we experience, we have within us an unquenchable spark and thirst for life. We are called and we are filled with a desire to be able to live above these things while still having to dwell among them. It is a

3

hurdle. It takes incomprehensible willpower and determination to take back our lives. Especially when it's minute by minute, day by day, and night by night. We fight for victory on the field of anguish. And we face a looming but not impossible predicament: How can we take away the power that pain has over our lives?

It requires a lot of trust in the Lord. It takes all of the trust that heaven provides. And if we can breathe in and jump in and live in that trust, we are emboldened. Let's get bold enough to give God a great big God-size chance. After all, He did create the Universe!

Trust that the Lord has a plan for your life. Trust that He hears your prayers. Place even more trust in the reality that He hears every prayer that is said for you. Every single word. How about trusting and trying this:

Lean into the Lord. Lean way, way into His

arms. Abandon all preconceived notions about pain and frustration. Acknowledge that your life is precious and vibrant. Allow the thought that within His plan for your life is liberation from pain. This trust, beloved, is the birthplace of peace in your heart.

Trust. Lean. Jump. Live!

"This is what the LORD, the God of
your father David, says: 'I have heard
your prayer and seen your tears; I
will heal you.'"
—2 Kings 20:5
NIV

Healed? Yes! Healed! Just what does that look
like to me? Does the meaning of the word
"healed" change as my health fluctuates? Lord, I
need You. I've quite forgotten who I am. Remind
me again that I am Yours. I belong to You.

Encourage me today to move and think in a
forward direction. With Your support, I will make

a list of the things that bring me pleasure, joy, and comfort. It's a list that shall grow and grow. When I feel used up and hopeless, I can hold this list in my hand and experience renewal.

Lord, I thank You for each glorious day. I know that my definition of healed and Yours may be quite different. Please show me how to surrender to You and Your plans for me.

> "Rejoice in hope, be patient in
> suffering, persevere in prayer."
> —Romans 12:12
> NRSV

This is a short course in how to live each day. Hold on to this verse when you just can't concentrate and when it seems impossible to tackle the day's "to do" list. If you're experiencing a pain flare or dealing with chronic fatigue, the number of days the "to do" list gets left behind can begin to stack up. At some point, it's easy to begin to feel diminished. The negative self-talk starts, and we question our capability and even our worth.

When you begin to believe that your value lies in what you're able to accomplish each day, it's time to sit down and talk to Jesus. Surrender the things of this world to Him. Take a moment and quiet your heart before Him. Breathe in His love and just let go. Hold this verse in your hand and let the words lead you forward. Maybe today you can do all three of these things. Maybe today you can do only one.

Breathe in His love. Just let go. Hold on to this verse.

You can always choose to have hope in your heart. Hope is the birthplace of joy.

If you can't be patient with your own situation, give the gift of patience to someone you love.

To persevere is to stop at nothing. And nothing can stop Jesus from getting you through today.

"Keep me safe, my God, for in you I
take refuge."
—Psalm 16:1
NIV

Where is your safe place when you feel devastated? Maybe your safe place is a memory. A memory of a time and place when your soul was quieted and nothing could harm you. Perhaps it is a place in nature, or the touch of a loved one. You can even create a safe place in your imagination.

When pain and frustration and the very thought of another doctor's appointment combine to overwhelm you, just close your eyes and travel.

Reminisce and remember sharing a spectacular sunset with a glass of wine and your very best friend. Maybe you hear your husband's laughter. What was the name of that beach where you wept while the sun set so gloriously and you felt awash in the colors of the Kingdom?

Where is your refuge?

Where would you like God to take you today?

The Search

In everything God has made

the sky

the flowers

the human face:

It is there we will see the

Glory of God.

Our friendships are a treasure box

overflowing with the

Gifts of God:

Grace

Patience

Love

Acceptance

Peace and

Companionship

While we are together

on this blessed place we call Earth,

let us mindfully

seek the

beauty and heart of Jesus

in each other.

We cherish God

when we find Him in each other's eyes.

Father God, Abba, thank You for the people You
place in our lives.

Today, especially, I want to thank You for:

> "I am the way, and the truth, and the
> life."
> —John 14:6
> **NRSV**

I woke up this morning with three things on my mind: The way. The truth. And the life.

Show me the way I can make a difference by telling the truth about the way You have worked in my life. You have given me a new strength, and I'm going to share that strength today. Open the windows to my heart and pull back the curtains of my soul, because I am done thinking about myself. Like a close-up camera lens, I begin to hone in on the faces and needs of other people. I already know my own story . . . it's time I learned a chapter or two about someone else who might be hurting. Your way, God, is truly a brand-new life.

Good things come in threes.

Father. Son. Holy Spirit.

The way. The truth. The life.

Open my ears.

Focus my eyes.

Give me Your voice.

> "How long must I wrestle with my
> thoughts and every day have sorrow
> in my heart?"
> —Psalm 13:2
> NIV

Take me away today, O LORD.
Take me to a place without
discord and tension.

Take me today, my God,
to a place where there is quiet,
where love flows amongst the thorns and hope is
always in bloom.

Speak to me this day, Abba.
Warm me with Your wisdom.

Gather me unto You, for You
are the promise of a love that never fails.
A love that always leads me safely back to
You.

Lead me, today, my Father
on a long and winding walk through
Your living, loving, thriving
Word.

Amen.

"No one tears a piece from a new garment and sews it on an old garment; otherwise the new will be torn, and the piece from the new will not match the old."

—Luke 5:36

NRSV

Good News! Christ is not finished working on us. It doesn't matter if we are in a hospital bed, a wheelchair, or in a physical body bound by disease or pain; the miracle of new creation never stops. VERY Good News! Jesus just doesn't patch up the holes in our Old Selves. He's not content with that. Oh, no! Remember, we are speaking of the Man who promised to make all things new.

Father God, instead of focusing on my physical self today, lead me to gaze upon Your Son, Jesus. Jesus can bring new life to my spirit, new growth to my faith, and all I have to do is ask.

Good News!

"Therefore we do not lose heart.
Though outwardly we are wasting
away, yet inwardly we are being
renewed day by day."
—2 Corinthians 4:16
NIV

You painted the canvas of the earth with a marvelous palette of colors that reflect the changing of seasons. Just like the seasons, I find that my relationship with my pain is ever changing. Sometimes I wonder, Lord, is it a privilege to be in pain? I ask because this pain leads me closer to You and I feel I grow more deeply in relationship with You in Your humanity.

When I feel my heart and my hope slipping away, I see a parade of the faces of pain. These faces are a collection of ugly mug shots. The face of fear. The face of anger. Faces of grief and sorrow. Like strangers on a crowded street, they jostle one another. They press on, endlessly, competing for center stage in the arena of my life. But those rare moments when I know I cannot bear another moment or take another breath, this thought hits me on a visceral level: *What I'm feeling is just a grain of sand compared to the pain My Savior endured.* I have a small opportunity to share in Your experience and emotions.

Reflection

Don't forget that there are countless other ways that Jesus gives each of us a glimpse of Himself every day. Where do you see Him at work in your life?

Prayer

Thank You, precious Jesus, for putting my attention and focus back where they need to be—on You, not me. Thank You for letting me see and live some of Your most intimate moments with the Father. Help me today to be like You. Open. Loving. Trusting. Peaceful. Amen.

"O Most High, when I am afraid, I put my trust in you. . . . You have kept count of my tossings; put my tears in your bottle. Are they not in your record?"
—Psalm 56:2, 8
NRSV

Creator, Sustainer, Redeemer, Beloved Provider. How comforting it is to visualize myself at Your feet. How soothing is Your presence. When we speak in prayer I sometimes physically feel You lift the burden of my anxiety from my shoulders. How many more tears would I shed if it were not for Your generosity and concern? Abba, I crawl into

Your lap like a little child. I am helpless and hopeless. But once I feel the comfort and nearness of You, everything changes.

My sorrows become Your sorrows. You take my tears into Yourself and I am no longer alone. You teach me that these tears serve a greater purpose. Gently and graciously, You show me that a renewed attitude will make me stronger. You speak in the night and teach me that each tear I shed creates more space in my heart. Cleansing. Opening. As the space in my heart increases, so does my capacity to experience joy. Joy in Your Word, joy in Your love, and joy in Your world. Joy for the family and friends You have given me. Gratitude for my caregivers and their unending generosity. It is all to Your glory.

Thanks be to You, Lord. Thanks be to You.

> "And I said: 'Here I am. Send me.'"
> —Isaiah 6:8
> NIV

Dear Lord: I greet this day with an open heart. I ask that You help me focus on others today. It is very easy for me to let another day just tick and tock around the clock until it's time for bed. I feel like I have allowed my pain to win yet another round. The only thing I accomplished today was experiencing self-pity. Truly and fully I entreat You, don't let me squander another day. Bestow Your Holy strength upon my spirit and help me sweep away my discomfort, my fear, and my doubt. Please open my eyes today and show me all the places I am needed. Yes, I can be Your hands and feet!

As I greet people today, even as I think about people today, give me a new focus; a focus that sharpens my sight, enabling me to see with the eyes and mind of a brand-spanking-new, fully remodeled, ready-to-serve-the-Lord creature. Let me seek You with the eyes of a servant.

May today be a day that I live in service. Let me be open to the needs of others instead of thinking of my own situation. Please give me the confidence and knowledge that You will travel with me today. I want—no, I crave—a chance to experience the joy that beats in the heart of a servant.

I know all of the equipment I will ever need to be a warrior for Christ resides in my heart. Lord of All Life, You are my conviction and my intention.

Thank you this day and every day for the opportunity to serve You by serving others.

Here I am, right here! Send me!

Reflection

Think of all the people who populate your life.
Where might you be needed today?

"He was praying in a certain place, and after he had finished, one of his disciples said to him, 'Lord, teach us to pray.'"
—Luke 11:1
NRSV

Prayer. His language. Our lifeline. Isn't it a miracle that the most understanding and tender counselor in the Universe is available to us twenty-four hours a day, seven days a week? Very often, I find that when I am praying for others I experience a release from the bondage of thinking about my own current quandary. Prayer can lift us high above the rut and desolation of chronic illness.

I believe the Lord sees some of our most precious "lifting" when we raise our brothers and sisters in prayer. It seems like such a small thing. A prayer can take just a few seconds. We can simply and silently entreat, trusting the Holy Spirit to interpret our intentions. I feel that Jesus appreciates our intercession. After all, in His time on Earth, Jesus did some pretty heavy "lifting," didn't He? His prayer muscles are divinely sculpted.

Prayer is a journey we undertake that will deepen the intimacy of our relationship with Christ. When we pray, we can find solace in His protection. When we pray, we are assured that He hears our appeals and promises His peace.

"Yet I am always with you; you hold me by my right hand. You guide me with your counsel, and afterward you will take me into glory. Whom have I in heaven but you? And the earth has nothing I desire besides you. My flesh and my heart may fail, but God is the strength of my heart and my portion forever."

—Psalm 73:23–26

NIV

How these words sing within me! The strength of these promises surrounds me with unlimited grace. It's a grace that dances in my heart and banishes all things dark. O, Father, how ardently I seek You in prayer! My soul leaps like a young gazelle. I bound toward You, unrestrained by the noise of the world around me. I am ever eager to hear Your voice. You speak to me with such soul sweetness, guiding me to a life lived close to You. Lord. God. King of the Universe. Creator of Heaven and Earth. You long to be with me. You, too, bask in our time together. Whatever on this Earth can compare to You?

Thank You for Your counsel. Thank You for all the things that You teach me. Thank You for never letting go of my hand.

You are:

My strength. My portion.

I love You.

"Your word is a lamp to my feet and
a light to my path."
—Psalm 119:105
NRSV

What joy! I awaken today strengthened by the knowledge Your Word will sustain me and guide me. When I am dark, Your word brings me light.

Please, Father, as we spend this quiet time together, give me the vision to see all of the blessings You bring to my life. I will write a list of these blessings on the tablet of my heart. Your gifts are life giving and generous. They include: Your

Son. My family. Your Living Word. My friends. The Counselor. Your peace. Your wisdom. Sunrise. Sunset. The autumn glow of towering trees and the sprouting renewal of my garden in the spring.

I sing Your praises.

I am sustained. In Your Word. In You. Gracious God.

You Spangle the Stars

Twilight lulls Your world to sleep.

Blue horizons turn velveteen grey

as evening lulls the swallows homeward . . .

Moving as one they arc,

spanning the horizon with their

grace in flight.

Darkness deepens

and You spangle the sky with Your stars:

An eternal testimony to the

Grandeur of Your majesty.

Oh Lord,

My Lord,

let me rest this evening

in the sanctuary of Your arms,

my arms reaching and beseeching that

I may reflect the

Glory of Your light.

Help me each day

to light the way.

Let me live in the

lesson of my life . . .

ever moving

ever growing

Carol K. Grosz

ever longing

to be Your pleasure.

> "The one who enters by the gate is
> the shepherd of the sheep ... He calls
> his own sheep by name and leads
> them out ... the sheep follow him
> because they know his voice."
> —John 10:2–4
> NRSV

The Gospel of John tells us the story of one anointed sheep that heard the Shepherd's voice very clearly. It tells us the story of Mary Magdalene. Following the death of Jesus, Mary stumbles her way to His tomb. Finding it empty, she is heartsick. She weeps from the depths of her being. She longs to know where to find the body of

Jesus. Seeing a man she believes to be the gardener, she literally cries: "They have taken my Lord away!" Slowly, this gardener turns to her and says just one word. He says her name. He says: "Mary."

Do you ever get so wrapped up in the reading of Scripture that you find yourself right in the middle of what's happening? I am always left with my heart beating and banging as I peek into this particular picture. I am there when she once again hears the Voice that gave her life grace and purpose. I listen, too. Surely He spoke softly and tenderly when He called to His lamb: "Mary." As I measure this moment, I have a question to ask you: Where were you when He called *your* name? What was happening in your life when you heard Him speak out to you in your brokenness? His voice was as clear as the ring of the telephone or a knock on the door. Where were you when you heard it: "Melanie . . . Rick . . . Ann . . . Phil . . ." Did you weep? Did you laugh with unfettered joy and freedom? Maybe you just allowed the tears to flow and the healing to commence. Where were you when He called your name?

Never stop listening, for Your Shepherd keeps His promises. He is always with you, and you are never alone.

"Be still and know that I am God."
—Psalm 46:10
NIV

Tonight I felt Your love fall all over and around me like the soft silhouette of winter's first midnight snowfall.

Tonight I tossed and turned for hours, unable to shed the heaviness of the day. Discomfort and dread. Dread and discomfort. Two all-too-familiar signposts on the map of my life. I searched my mind and heard the unmistakable sound of unwanted thoughts and familiar worries. Yes, Lord, I know how to worry. I know how to feel forgotten. Yet tonight, I thought, tonight can be different.

Tonight can be different. If only I could just be still. Just for one moment and then for one moment more.

Quieting my thumping heart, I take in a deep, purposeful breath of You. Your peace. Your serenity. Your promise.

You're here . . .

"Get thee behind me, Satan!"
—Mark 8:33
NRSV

The Enemy has no power against Jesus. Our Lord does not allow Satan to walk alongside Him. He would never allow Satan to lead. With Satan planted firmly behind Him, Jesus stands between His children and the enemy. Christ is a spiritual guardian that Satan cannot pass. The Evil One is a master manipulator. He uses every trick in his arsenal to make us believe that we are without hope. He would be jubilant if he could entice us to walk the corridors of sadness, self-pity, anger, and frustration. However,

Satan has one problem: he cannot get past Our Guardian Lord!

The next time you feel as though the road to nowhere is straight ahead . . . just tell Satan where to go!

Behind you!

Prayer

Precious Jesus, You defeated Satan in life. Everlasting Lord, You defeated him in death. Thank You, my Holy Champion. Because You defend me, I will not give in today. With the eyes of my heart, I now envision You standing in front of me, protecting me from darkness. I lay my gratitude and love at the foot of Your Cross.

Amen.

Angels

To the angels we know and the ones we have
yet to meet

I've always wondered

if angels really fly.

I wonder if they live on Earth.

I wonder if angels are

tall and blonde and if they have blue eyes.

I wonder if

they are short and swarthy

with a mop of curly pirate's hair.

Where would I,

where could I look?

Can I even find and see an angel?

Perhaps in a dress that reaches across the years,

or in a photo family album

across the street,

or maybe, just maybe,

angels live inside a memory.

If I could touch an angel,

could an angel touch me back?

I always wonder

where your

wings are hidden.

I want an angel to touch me today.

"Your righteousness reaches to the skies, O God, you who have done great things. Who, O God, is like you? Though you have made me see troubles, many and bitter, you will restore my life again; from the depths of the earth you will bring me up. You will increase my honor and comfort me once again."
—Psalm 71:19–21
NIV

These words teach me that, ultimately, I need to be ready to rely upon God all day long. I must trust His plan. I have long lived with the combined stress of pain and disappointment and managed to continue to be productive. I can do it again today. With God at my side, there is no reason I cannot accomplish living a restored life each day. As I read these words I pray:

Father: Send me to my knees. It is when I'm on my knees that I see the door to Your schoolroom is wide open. Like the psalmist before me, I long to hear You speak to my heart. Give me rest in the assurance that You never will leave me, no matter how dire the circumstances of the world may become. You will always, always reach down from Heaven and lift me up. Thank You, my Lord. Thank You for the promises of "forever" and "always" that live in Your Word.

"Create in me a clean heart, O God, and put a new and right spirit within me. Do not cast me away from your presence and do not take your holy spirit from me. Restore to me the joy of your salvation and sustain in me a willing spirit."
—Psalm 51:10–12
NRSV

Father. Abba. King of the Universe: Without a heart cleansed of pessimistic thoughts and intentions, a right spirit will not and cannot flourish within me. So many days, Lord, I need my spirit renewed. I wish this not just for myself, Father, but to enable me to serve others who may no longer hear Your voice and see the movement of Your Holy Spirit. Help me to help, Father.

Strengthen me to walk beyond what my body can do today. I ask You to help me reinforce, deep down in my being, that I can still touch hearts and minds, even when I can't leave my bed.

It's all about letting You work through me. I surrender to that right now and I let go of any reservations I have about being able to serve You.

I close my eyes and think of the marvelous deeds You have done in my life. My spirit leaps at the chance to share with others the joy of Your salvation.

Instruct this willing spirit, for I am Yours!

"I therefore, the prisoner in the Lord, beg you to lead a life worthy of the calling to which you have been called, with all humility and gentleness, with patience, bearing with one another in love, making every effort to maintain the unity of the Spirit in the bond of peace."
—Ephesians 4:1–3
NRSV

Thank You, Father, for reminding me to serve the people who are my caregivers. As I sit quietly with these words, I see You are gently leading me to a new way of life. It can be easy for the person who is ill to become just a little bit selfish. God, are You suggesting that maybe, perhaps, some- how, somewhere, there is something more im- portant, more pressing than "me" taking place? O, Father, You know I didn't mean to end up this way! My face is red and my heart is full of embar- rassment and shame. I don't want this.

O, Father, give me the grace to put myself aside and instead give my heart a great thirst for everyone I love dearly. Show me, God. Direct me to their needs so that I may be a positive force in their lives. Help me to be a messenger that bears tidings of gratitude for their gentle patience. Make me an overflowing vessel of love and unity and peace when I interact with each caregiver today. Attune me to their needs. I want to return to them all of the gentleness, patience, and love they have poured over me.

Thank You for Your Spirit of peace.

In recognition of a rare

treasure: friends

All the tears

in all the world

ofttimes wash

through the river of my heart.

And ofttimes all the

pain and all the sorrow in my body

strive to silence the

Song of the Spirit that flows through my soul.

Yet here in this season of my life

a voice rings out and a hand reaches for me.

It is you, my dear and treasured friend.

God has seasoned us, fostered us, and led us
forward

as we traveled through life.

He's been watching and reaping

and shaping and sowing

until He was certain

our hands fit together.

Thank you for walking beside me.

Thank you for the gift of your friendship.

> "It is I, do not be afraid."
> —John 6:20
> NRSV

It is not a stretch to compare a battle with illness to a major storm. The skies darken parts of our lives once filled with sunshine. We ache and we mourn the loss and surrender of beloved activities. The tears can fall as fast and heavy as the skies that move a storm front across the mountains. But, Child, take heart.

Don't forget about Jesus and the Message of the Cross. Do not forget that He gave His life to be with us always. All ways. He is always present.

Jesus walked across those crashing waves in the dead, deep dark of night to prove that nothing can stop Him from getting to us. Amen and Amen! He reassured us that we are never beyond His reach. We need only call His name and listen . . .

"Don't be afraid, it's Me. I'm right here."

> "Turn to me and be gracious to me;
> for I am lonely and afflicted."
> —Psalm 25:16
> NIV

I know lonely. I know afflicted. It's the gracious that I can't find in my life.

Speak to me, Spirit, and teach me a new vocabulary. I want to consciously choose words that are positive and affirming. I want a Spirit-filled pencil with a great big God-sized eraser to help me banish the pessimistic and counterproductive words I use to describe myself.

So, it's out with the negative and in with the

positive. Just watch the positive begin to shine. I will use that Spirit-filled pencil to write down all of the sparkling and promising new words in my vocabulary.

Let's go, Lord. Come on, Holy Spirit! Let's write something new about my life. Let's begin with A for affirming and work our way to Z for zeal!

Good Morning, Glory!

God has something for me to do today that only I can accomplish. He has something to say that requires my voice. I have to be in concert with Him. I have to be listening to Him. For Him. Right now He is asking me to make my voice just a little bit louder. Just a little bit. He's asking me to stand up just a little bit taller. Just a little bit. Today, God has a life that needs to be touched, and that means my hands need to get busy. Just a little bit busy.

I need to stop worrying about whether what I

do is going to be big enough. I need to quit wor-rying that my voice isn't going to be loud enough or strong enough or anything enough . . . because God's got this.

My willing heart is the only thing God needs to get this job done today.

Reflection

What has God put on your heart's to-do list today?

"Teach me good judgment and knowledge, for I believe in your commandments. Before I was humbled I went astray, but now I keep your word."
—Psalm 119:66–67
NRSV

I love this reading, Father, for it aptly describes our time together. You teach me something of value every time I open Your Word and spend time in Your presence. As the seasons in my life change, You lead me throughout the Bible and there is always a signpost, a story, or a word that speaks to my present situation.

I woke up this morning believing a lie. I thought because I am in pain that today wouldn't count. I told myself that because my body hurts and my mind is restless that You must have abandoned me and taken away my hope. But those are lies.

Father, teach me today one important lesson. Teach me not to quantify my days. Help me with vocabulary, Lord. Take away the words that suck the meaning out of my activities: "If only I felt better today, _____ would have been so much better." "When I'm stronger, I will be better at _____." Stop me when my mind takes this downward turn. Life humbled me when I could no longer pursue the career that was my passion. Life humbled me when I could no longer participate in the hobbies that brought me great pleasure.

Life humbled me when I could no longer walk to the bathroom and had to ask for help.

God, You already delight in my activities and me. You do not care how many steps I take today. You care only that I have faith in You and follow where You lead.

Help this humble servant bring Your Word to the world today!

> "I lie down and sleep; I wake again,
> for the Lord sustains me."
> —Psalm 3:5
> NRSV

Dear Lord in Heaven, pour out Your precious love upon my weary soul tonight. I beg of You to call upon the angels of Hope and Compassion. Bid them to open their wings and lift the weight of this day. This day has taken a mighty toll. My body and heart teeter on the edge of exhaustion.

Father, I need the rest and sustenance that only Your love can provide.

Lead me gently to this night's sleep. Let the

promise of a better tomorrow meet my head upon the pillow. I trust in this promise. I will lie down and seek my rest in the peace and security of Your arms.

I will rise again tomorrow secure in the knowledge that Your strength abides within me.

Amen.

> "Make a joyful noise to the LORD,
> all the earth. Worship the LORD with
> gladness; come into his presence
> singing."
> —Psalm 100:1–2
> NRSV

O, Light of the World, Lamb of God, Bright Morning Star:

Come alongside me, I beseech You this new day. Today I will live my life like a song of thanks and praise. Turn up the volume in my heart until my lungs are so full of You that this holy racket shakes the rafters on my roof and wakes up the neighbors!

Let there be joy!

Let's dance today, Jesus. I shed the concerns of this earthly body and throw open the door to the dance of life.

Sing it! Ring it! Bring it on!

Falling for Jesus

As I walked this morning, I watched a gentle breeze tumble and toss the autumn leaves. Some were dry and crackled. Some still boasted a brilliant red and orange, flaunting their scarlet hues as they moved with the wind. These same leaves had been tiny buds just a few months ago . . . tender and vulnerable. As the season progressed, the leaves opened fully and provided a dapple of shade or perhaps camouflage for a nest of bluebirds. Never questioning, these leaves move through birth, adulthood, death, and renewal. The work of our

Heavenly Artist is always glorious! On this sunlit warm morning, I look at the leaves and my heart is filled with a wish. I wish that I could surrender my heart to Jesus and fall into the rhythm of the life He has planned for me. What attachments keep me from following the Holy Spirit with reckless abandon? What makes me pause when I hear His voice in my heart, but unlike the leaf I hang on to the branches of my life? How would it look, how might it be, if I gave Jesus a chance to move me without question? What would those seasons look like in my life? Maybe I'm afraid of the uncertainty. Maybe I'm afraid my faith is not sufficient. Maybe I'm afraid of letting go.

In this journey of ever seeking healing, we should just try being a leaf. Instead of working so hard and trying so hard and constantly striving for positivity, we could just give Jesus a chance to make us new. Some of our fears may die and be reborn as hope. Some of our goals may be renewed if we can only relax into His holy hands.

What is it that holds you back today? What are you afraid of today? When you search your soul, what does your renewed life look like? Think about these things. Ponder them in your heart. Write them down and pray over them.

Jesus said: "Behold, I make all things new." All things means me and you!

Reflection

_____

_____

_____

_____

_____

_____

_____

_____

_____

_____

_____

_____

_____

_____

_____

_____

_____

_____

_____

_____

_____

_____

_____

_____

_____

_____

_____

_____

_____

_____

_____

Carol K. Grosz

_____

_____

_____

_____

_____

_____

_____

_____

_____

_____

_____

_____

_____

_____

_____

_____

_____

_____

_____

_____

_____

_____

_____

_____

_____

_____

_____

_____

_____

_____

_____

_____

_____

Carol K. Grosz

_____

_____

_____

_____

_____

_____

_____

_____

_____

_____

_____

_____

_____

_____

_____

_____

_____

_____

_____

_____

_____

_____

_____

_____

_____

_____

_____

_____

_____

_____

_____

_____

_____

Carol K. Grosz

Carol K. Grosz

About the Author

Carol K. Grosz is a retired Medical Massage Therapist who treated a wide variety of patients struggling with major medical challenges. From children with head injuries to Olympic medal–winning athletes who needed to perform at their highest level, she feels her patients were her best teachers. Carol served her patients while living with Chronic Regional Pain Syndrome. She was diagnosed with this condition twenty-seven years ago and remains dedicated to making a difference. She believes that her faith, especially her relationship with Jesus, is the foundation of her optimism, strength, and continued hope. A retreat facilitator, prayer advocate, and motivational speaker, Carol finds fulfillment walking beside her fellow Chronic Pain Warriors.

Her husband, Sandor, her sister, Jeri, and a community of loving friends sustain her. Lilli and Joey the Boston terriers round out her support team. A Midwest original, Carol now lives in the Atlanta area.

9 781631 835292